Anonymous

List of Ancient Monuments in the Dacca Division

Anonymous

List of Ancient Monuments in the Dacca Division

ISBN/EAN: 9783337384999

Printed in Europe, USA, Canada, Australia, Japan

Cover: Foto ©ninafisch / pixelio.de

More available books at **www.hansebooks.com**

Government of Bengal.

PUBLIC WORKS DEPARTMENT

LIST OF ANCIENT

IN THE

DACCA DIVISION

Revised and corrected up to

PUBLISHED BY A

Calcutta:
PRINTED AT THE BENGAL SECRETARIAT PRESS.
1896.

DACCA DIVISION.

4. DACCA

CLASSIFI

(See Government of India, Home Department.

I.—Those monuments which, from their present condition and historical or
II.—Those monuments which it is now only possible or desirable to save
the exclusion of water from the walls, and the like.
III.—Those monuments which, from their advanced stage of decay or

I. (a) and II (a).—Monuments in the possession or charge of Government, conservation.
I. (b) and II (b).—Monuments in the possession or charge of private

(1) DACCA

No.	District.	Locality.	Name of monument.	History or tradition regarding the monument.
1	2	3	4	5
1	Dacca	Dacca	Lálbágh Fort	This was commenced in 1678 by Sultán Muhammad Azam, third son of Aurangzeb, but was never finished. The old gateways and battlements still remain. They form a very picturesque feature in the landscape when viewed from the river which washes one solid bastion.
			Bibi Peri's Mausoleum.	Situated within the Lálbágh enclosure. It was erected towards the end of the 17th century by Nawab Shaista Khán, successor of Sultán Muhammad Azam, in memory of the Nawab's daughter, Bibi Peri, wife of Muhammad Azam. The tomb lies within a building which has a vaulted roof of sandstone slabs, and an ornamented floor of marble and basalt; its walls are of brick faced inside with marble. The central dome is protected outside by a covering of sheet copper. The building is one of architectural importance and is unique in Lower Bengal. There is a two-storied building in the middle of the Lálbágh Fort, apparently of ancient date. It has stone pillars and vaulted roof.
2	Do.	Do.	Husseni Dalan Palace.	It is said to have been built by Moer Morad, Superintendent of Public Buildings, in the time of Sultán Muhammad Azam.
			Tomb of Nawab Nasarat-jang. Tomb of Nawab Samsadwala. Tomb of Nawab Kamaradawala, son of the former. Tomb of Nawab Gasiuddin Hyder, son of the former.	These Nawabs died in the beginning of the 19th century. Their graves lie in one building situated within the compound of the Husseni Dalan. They have no inscriptions.

DIVISION.

CATION.

[Resolution No. 3—168—63, dated 20th November 1883.]

archæological value, ought to be maintained in permanent good repair.
from further decay by such minor measures as the eradication of vegetation,
comparative unimportance, it is impossible or unnecessary to preserve—
or in respect of which Government must undertake the cost of all measures of
bodies or individuals.

DISTRICT.

Custody or present use.	Present state of preservation and suggestions for conservation.	Classification.	REMARKS.
6	7	8	9
Used as a Police Tháná	The old gateways and battlements are in bad condition, being overgrown with jungle and trees and much affected by the action of saltpetre. They need preservation and require urgent repair.	iia	See pages 127 to 131 of Vol. XV of the Archæological Survey Reports. See also pages 66-67 of Hunter's Statistical Account of the Dacca district. Bishop Heber visited Dacca in July 1824.
......	Well worthy of preservation. Some repairs are needed to it, which should be carried out.	ia	
Is now occupied by the Police Department as a tháná.	Is in good condition, being maintained by the Public Works Department.	ia	
Used for religious ceremonies, especially in the Muharram. Government assumed charge of it, which has been delegated to Nawab Ashannullah, C.I.E., to whom Government pays an annual grant, which the Nawab largely supplements from his private funds.	Is in course of thorough renovation by the Nawab of Dacca from the Government grant supplemented by himself.	ia	
These tombs are under the custody of Nawab Ashannullah, C.I.E.	The building is in good condition and is maintained and repaired at the expense of Government, through Nawab Ashannullah, C.I.E., to whom an annual grant, dating from before British times, is continued by Government.	ia	

(1) DACCA

No.	District	Locality	Name of monument	History or tradition regarding the monument.
1	2	3	4	5
3	Dacca	Dacca	The chak (market place).	The chief market place of Dacca; is surrounded by a low enclosure wall. There is a mammoth cannon in the centre of very great antiquity raised upon a masonry pedestal.
4	Do.	Do.	Idgah of Mír Abdul Kásim.	This is a lofty masonry wall with prayer niches standing on the western part of the town near the Pílkhána. It was built in 1640 by Mír Abdul Kásim, household Diwán of Sultán Sujah.
5	Do.	Do.	Great Katra (caravanserai).	This was built by Mír Abdul Kásim Khán under the orders of the Prince Azimushan during the latter's Viceroyalty of Bengal in the year 1645 A.D. It is said that it was intended for travellers and was to serve the purpose of a caravanserai. It is a building of enormous massiveness and solidity, and will not rapidly fall into decay. The building from its dimensions looks imposing from the river; the main gateway facing the river is picturesque. On its completion the Prince inspected it, but did not like it, and gave it to Mír Abdul Kásim.
6	Do.	Do.	Small Katra (caravanserai).	This was built by Amiral Omrah, Nawab Shaistá Khán, on his succeeding prince Azimushan as Viceroy of Bengal. It is said that it was intended for a caravanserai and was built some years after the great Katra, but the exact year is not known. It looks well from the river having one fine doorway facing in that direction.
7	Do.	Do.	Temple of Dhákeśvarí.	A Hindu temple, of considerable celebrity, sacred to the goddess of Dacca (Dhákeśvarí). This is the temple of the tutelary deity of Dacca, and is according to the local tradition very ancient.
8	Do.	Ditto (Shahbag, a Park of the Nawab's north of Dacca.)	Tomb	This is an old tomb in a park belonging to Nawab Asbanullah, C.I.E., of Dacca. Nothing is known about the history of the tomb or the person interred within it. The building which contains the tomb is a quadrangular hall on a low plinth, with the grave in its centre built in masonry. The hall measures 25' × 18' and is open on all sides and supported by rectangular pillars spanned by semicircular arches. The hall is roofed over by a vault with a small rise, so that the building looks flat-roofed from outside. The whole outer face of the building is covered with ornamental work in plaster.
9	Do.	Dacca (Ramná)	Mosque of Háji Kahjeh Shahabag.	This mosque is said to have been built 200 years ago by Háji Kahjeh Shahabag, a merchant of Káshmír. It is said that he originally came from that place and settled in the town of Dacca, where he prospered in trade. The mosque, which stands on the S.-W. of Ramná, is a quadrangular building of brick masonry 67' × 26' on the outside, roofed over with three domes, and ornamented at the corners with eight minarets, which are

DISTRICT—continued.

Custody or present use.	Present state of preservation and suggestions for conservation.	Classification.	REMARKS.
6	7	8	9
Market is held every afternoon within the enclosure.	The wall is in a bad state of repair.	iii	
In custody of the local Muhammadans. Still used for religious ceremonies during the Id festival.	It requires repairs	ib	
In private hands; pretty well looked after.	Nearly if not quite intact and not likely easily to fall into decay.	iib	
It is in private hands and is pretty well looked after.	It is substantial and not likely easily to fall into decay.	iib	
......	Has been lately repaired and is in good condition, the recent repairs having greatly improved its state.	ib	
In custody of Nawab ...	Good. The Nawab has lately repaired it.	iib	
It is under the custody of Jaga Shah Sáheb of Muhalla Beobárám Dewri, Dacca, who looks after the mosque and provides it with lights and mats. It is still used as a place of worship.	The plaster and the ornamental work have decayed, and vegetation and trees have grown over the building. To carry out thorough repairs a sum of Rs. 1,000 is needed.	iii	

(1) DACCA

No.	District.	Locality.	Name of monument.	History or tradition regarding the monument.
1	2	3	4	5
			Tomb of Háji Kahjeh Shahabag.	mostly broken. The outside course of the plinth at the level of the floor is built of long blocks of basalt, carved in the shape of a neat fringe. The door frames are also of basalt. There are three doors on the eastern, i.e., the front, side of the mosque and one each on the north and the south sides. The door openings have neat pointed arches. The masonry of the whole structure, though very old, is strong. Attached to the mosque and close to it lies the tomb of its founder, Háji Kahjeh Shahabag. It is said that the mosque and the tomb were built at one and the same time by their founder, and that after his death his body was interred within the tomb. The building which contains the tomb is a square one measuring 20' outside and surmounted by a single dome and four minarets.
10	Dacca	Dacca (Thatari Bazar).	Temples of Jayakáli and Siva.	These temples are of considerable celebrity. The centre temple is a small terrace-roofed building 22' x 20' dedicated to the God Siva with two large temples on each side. In it is the image of the goddess Káli, a very fine specimen of sculpture in stone. Of the side temples the western one is a "Panchoratna," or a temple with five towers, of which the centre one is about 50 feet high, with side ones of a smaller height. The eastern temple stands on a base 12 feet square and rises in a single spire to a height of about 70 feet, and it can be seen from a great distance. The temples are of very solid construction, and ornamented outside with carved work in brick and plaster. They are about 200 years old. There stood close by an older temple called "Navaratna," which was 250 years old and which collapsed about 12 years ago. The railway line now runs close in front of the temples which stand up picturesquely as viewed from the train.
11	Do.	Ditto (Armenian Street.)	Armenian Church of the Holy Resurrection.	In the early part of the eighteenth century, the Armenians settled at Dacca in Eastern Bengal and formed a colony there, when it was one of the important commercial centres in Bengal. There they flourished in commercial pursuits for a considerable time, and amassed great riches. At first they built a small chapel, where they worshipped prior to the erection of the present church, and they lie buried in the cemetery at Tejgaon, where many an old tombstone with Armenian inscriptions can be seen. The oldest is to the memory of one Avetis, an Armenian merchant, who had died at Dacca on 15th August 1714. In 1781 the growing community erected the present Armenian church at Dacca in the locality known as Armanitola (Armenian Street) and dedicated it to the "Holy Resurrection." The ground was the gift of Agah Catchick Minas, and on it stood the small chapel already referred to.

DISTRICT—continued.

Custody or present use.	Present state of preservation and suggestions for conservation.	Classification.	REMARKS.
6	7	8	9
In custody of the local Muhammadans.	The building which contains the tomb is much overgrown with trees and damaged in many places. The vestibule, which had a fine gabled arch of brick masonry, has fallen in. The necessary repairs can be carried out at a cost of Rs. 500.	ib	
The temples are resorted to by large numbers of people as a place of worship. There was once some landed property attached to them, but it has now been alienated for want of proper deed of gift.	The temples are very old and are overgrown with vegetation and trees. If the jungle were eradicated, the plaster renewed and the walls whitewashed, they would last for a long while. The cost of such repairs may be estimated at about 500 rupees, which it is not in the power of the present custodian of the temples to defray.	iib	
In use as a church, and is in the custody of a warden.	In good order ...	ib	See pages 151-152 of the *History of the Armenians in India* by Mesrovb J. Seth, Armenian Examiner to the University of Calcutta.

(8)

(1) DACCA

No.	District.	Locality.	Name of monument.	History or tradition regarding the monument.
1	2	3	4	5
				In the early part of the present century the most eminent Armenian merchant and zemindar of Dacca was the famous Agah Arratoon Michael, who died a millionaire in 1824. The founder of the Dacca Pogose School, Mr. Nicholas Pogose, was another rich Armenian zemindar of Dacca. That once-flourishing colony is reduced to a few families only, as in the case of Bombay and Madras. The church contains some ancient inscriptions.

There is an unfinished clock tower on the west of the Armenian church, under which are the graves of Hiripsimiah, who died on 15th February 1837, and of her husband Johanness Carrapiet Sarkies, who died 25th January 1854. After his wife's death, Mr. Sarkies erected in July 1837 a tower of small height upon the present base with a large bell. The bell broke in 1860 or 1861; Mr. Sarkies then had the bell tower broken down, indented for a large clock from England, and commenced building the present clock tower over the old walls of the bell tower. The work was delayed owing to mismanagement till Mr. Sarkies lost his reason, and subsequently died. The clock with his other properties was sold off after his death; the tower is still standing in an unfinished state. Though not of any antiquity, it is a conspicuous and interesting object in Dacca. Proposals are on foot for its completion by the Armenian residents of the place. |
| 12 | Dacca | ... | Dacca (Cemetery) | Tomb of Colombo Saheb. | This is a lofty mausoleum situated near the tomb of the Joseph Paget, and is an octagonal building with a dome on the top. The inside measurement of each of the sides of the octagonal base is 5'-6". The height from floor to the highest point of the ceiling of the dome is about 40 feet, and the total height from the base to the ridge is about 46'. The structure is divided into three stages. The first or lower portion is 14 feet in height from the plinth. There are four doorways in it, each measuring 2'-8" by 6'-0"; there are also recesses on the remaining four sides measuring 4'-6" by 12'-0". There is an ordinary simple cornice on top of the first stage. The second or middle stage is also about 14' in height, and there are eight windows, one on each side, measuring 3'-6" by 8'-0"; these are fitted up with ornamental earthenware louvre work. There is a cornice on top of this stage like the one described for the first stage. The last stage or the top portion is a dome or cupola 12 feet in height. At each corner of the octagon there is an octagonal pillar on the outside surmounted by a vase like that generally to be found in Muhammadan mosques. There are also four pillars on the four corners of the circumscribed square, and these look like ordinary buttresses. There are three graves inside the structure without any inscriptions. |

DISTRICT—continued.

Custody or present use.	Present state of preservation and suggestions for conservation.	Classification.	REMARKS.
6	7	8	9
......	It is overgrown with trees and has cracked in some places.	i*b*	
The building is in the charge of the Public Works Department.	In good order ...	i*a*	See page 199 of Vol. I of Bishop Heber's Journals: London, 1828.

(1) DACCA

No.	District.	Locality.	Name of monument.	History or tradition regarding the monument.
1	2	3	4	5
13	Dacca	Dacca	Páglá bridge...	On the 5th mile of the Dacca-Náráyangañj road, probably erected by Mir Jumlá, who became Viceroy of the Dacca province in 1660.
14	Do.	Do.	Tungi bridge...	On the 14th mile of the Dacca-Mymensingh road. Probably erected by the same Viceroy as the above, the style of architecture being very similar. The bridge was blown up by order of the Magistrate of Dacca during the Mutiny. An engraving in Sir C. D'Oyly's Ruins of Dacca shows that one arch had fallen in many years before. A new iron bridge was built, but was carried away by the extraordinary high flood of 1890.
15	Do.	Karánigañj (6 miles west of Dacca).	The Sát Gomal mosque.	This mosque is situated on the extreme edge of very high land on the borders of a deep and large swamp and is very picturesque. Strong revetment walls support the mosque on the west side, i.e., towards the swamp. There is a small enclosed courtyard in front of it, but the enclosure walls have fallen down, and the gateway is in ruins. There are other minor mosques and tombs in the vicinity, but they are in ruins and without any inscriptions, and no history of them can be traced.
				No history can either be traced showing the age or the founder of the Sát Gomal Mosque; there is no stone inscription or anything connected with the mosque which might give a clue to its history. The Mollah says that there was an engraved stone built over the central doorway of the mosque, but that when it was neglected and overgrown with jungle the stone was detached from the building and taken away by mischievous persons.
				The masjid is an oblong hall 48' x 16' feet inside measurement with four hollow, octagonal towers of 8' inside and 12' outside measurement. These are in two stories and are surmounted each by a dome. The main hall is also roofed over by three domes in the usual mosque fashion, and these three domes with the four others on the corner towers make in all seven in number, which give rise to the name of Sát Gomal Masjid, or the mosque of 7 domes. The building is ornamented both inside and outside with innumerable niches and recesses.
16	Do.	Mirpur, thána Keránigañj.	Tomb of Shah Ali Sáheb.	About 8 miles to the north-west of the town of Dacca, near the large village of Mirpur stands the Dargá or the Mausoleum of the saint Shah Ali Sáheb. It is a square building 36 feet outside measurement and about the same in height with walls 7 feet thick and contains the tomb of the saint in its centre. The walls are surmounted by a single large tower with four small minarets at its corners. Over the central doorway are two stone inscriptions, one in

DISTRICT—*continued.*

Custody or present use.	Present state of preservation and suggestions for conservation.	Classification.	REMARKS.
6	7	8	9
Abandoned, a new bridge having been erected about 50 feet east of it.	The bridge is in a dilapidated condition; the turrets which flanked it still stand on the banks. A very picturesque ruin.	iii	See page 202 of Vol. I of Bishop Heber's Journals: London, 1828.
Abandoned	Remnants of the old structure are still standing.	iii	See footnote on page 121 of Hunter's Statistical Account of the Dacca district.
Under the charge of the local Muhammadans.	It was thoroughly reclaimed and repaired by Nawab Sir Abdul Gunny, K.C.S.I., about eight years ago, and it stands in every respect a practically new building. He also pays a monthly donation towards the maintenance of a priest who enjoys the produce of a piece of rent-free land of about 12 pakhis in area.	ii*b*	
It is still used as a place of worship, not only by the local Muhammadans, but by those coming from distant places.	The Dargá is in good repair and is patronised by Nawab Sir Abdul Gunny, K.C.S.I., who has but lately added a mosque for prayers, a small building for itinerant "fakirs" or Muhammadan devotees and an enclosed building for the use of zanana ladies coming to offer their	ii*b*	

(12)

(1) DACCA

No.	District.	Locality.	Name of monument.	History or tradition regarding the monument.
1	2	3	4	5
				Tughra Arabic and the other in ornamental Persian character. Ink impressions of both these inscriptions have been sent to the Government Epigraphist. Nothing very particular is known in the neighbourhood about the saint. The current tradition is that about 400 years ago Shah Ali, a prince of Bagdad, having renounced the pleasures of the world, came with four disciples and lived in a small mosque at this place. He ordered his disciples not to disturb him in his devotions for 16 months and shut himself up in the mosque for the performance of penances without any food or refreshments. The time passed, and when only one day remained the curiosity of the disciples was excited by a noise within as if of some liquid boiling over a fire. They forced open the door and found nothing remaining of the saint except a pool of boiling blood. They remained transfixed when an aërial voice in the tones of the saint ordered them to inter the blood as his remains at the spot, which they did. The place became famous for its sanctity, and ever since pilgrims have been flocking in large numbers to offer their prayers before the tomb. Some time after his interment an unknown merchant, who made large profits in his business in the neighbourhood, attributing his fortunes to the mediation of the saint, built this present Dargá or Mausoleum on the spot.
17	Dacca	Naliganj (Náráyanganj).	Kadam Rasul Fort and mosque.	This fort is traditionally supposed to contain a print of the prophet's foot, hence the name. The mosque said to contain the footprint is in fair condition. The two-storeyed gateway facing the river is a striking building.
18	Do.	Hájiganj	Fort	This fort was erected by the Viceroy, Mir Jumlá, to resist the incursions of the Mughs and Arakanese.
19	Do.	Munshiganj	Fort	This fort was built during the time of the Emperor Aurangzeb for protecting the country from the invasion of the Burmese. Within the enclosure wall are situated the residence of the Subdivisional Officer of Munshiganj and the lock-up, the first of which is built upon the top of the chief bastion.
20	Do.	Sonakhanda	Fort ruins	This fort is situated at the junction of the Lakhya and Dhalesvari rivers. It stands opposite Náráyanganj on the east side of the Lakhya river. It is one of the three forts built for the purpose of repelling the invasions of the Mughs and Arakanese. It is a level quadrangular space measuring 296′ × 190′ surrounded by a wall of brickwork 10 feet in height with inner and intermediate bastions and a raised outwork on the western face. The wall is

(13)

DISTRICT—*continued.*

Custody or present use.	Present state of preservation and suggestions for conservation.	Classification.	REMARKS.
6	7	8	9
	prayers at the Dargá. He also keeps up a garden and a small tank in connection with the Dargá, pays for a permanent guard, and offers regular donations for the festival occasions. He has also constructed two roads, one leading from the Juspar river and the other from the Dacca-Goalundo road to the Dargá, and has thus made the place formerly embedded in jungle accessible both by land and water.		
In private hands and much frequented by the Muhammadans of the district.	Is in good order, having been lately thoroughly renovated. The surrounding walls are dilapidated, but of no interest.	iii	
Belongs to Nawab Ashanullah, C.I.E. Has been utilised by the Nawab as the basis of a new building	The exterior walls of the fort and a bastion are standing.	iii	
It is under the custody of Government.	The enclosure wall and five bastions are still standing. These are in bad condition and are overgrown with trees and jungle and need repair, the cost of which will be about Rs. 1,000.	ia	
Is in private hands and is the joint property of the local zemindars.	In a totally ruined state, being overgrown with pipal trees. The outwork in the front is in a ruined condition, and the conservation of the structure is impossible.	iii	

(1) DACCA

No.	District.	Locality.	Name of monument.	History or tradition regarding the monument.
1	2	3	4	5
	Dacca	Sonárgaon or Savarnagrám.	......	loop-holed for 3 feet from the top, the bottom being built solid. It is only 8½ feet thick, and though standing for the most part, it is in a totally ruined state, being overgrown with pipal trees. The Lakhya river must at one time have flowed by the foot of the fort, but it is now about 300 feet distant.
				This is in the Náráyanganj subdivision. It was the capital of a Hindu principality anterior to the invasion of Muhammad Bakhtiyar Khiliji, A.D. 1203. Coins have been discovered on which Sonárgaon is designated "Hazrati Jalal," a title afterwards given to Mozimábád, which was made the mint city. During the 15th and part of the 16th centuries, Sonárgaon was the capital of an independent monarchy. About the 16th century, the city swarmed with pirs, fakirs, and other religious mendicants to a greater extent than perhaps any other Indian city. Amidst the ruins and forests of modern Sonárgaon it is said that at least 150 "geddis" of fakirs are distinguishable.
				The following is a description of the old buildings of Sonárgaon.
21	Do.	Ditto (S.-W. of Moulla Baghalpur.)	Tombs of five Pírs (saints).	The sepulchres of the five pirs are placed parallel to one another, and are raised about four feet from the ground. The river Brahmaputra must in former days have flowed past them. It was at one time intended to cover the tombs with a roof, but the pillars were never raised more than a few feet. The age of these graves, the names of the holy men, and the country whence they came are unknown. The belief is that they came from the west. At the south-west corner of the enclosure is a small uninteresting mosque, which, like the tombs, is rapidly falling into ruins.
				This dargá is considered so sacred that even Hindus aslám as they pass, and Muhammadan pilgrims resort to it from great distances. There are only two other shrines to which Muhammadans make pilgrimages in Eastern Bengal,—one is the tomb of Shah Ali Shahib at Mírpur, a few miles north-west of Dacca; the other is the dargá of Pír Badar Auliga, at Chittagong. The latter is the patron saint of all Hindu and Muhammadan boatmen and fishermen in Eastern Bengal.
22	Do.	Ditto	Tomb of Ghyasuddin Asam Shah.	About five hundred yards south-east of the above dargá, on the edge of a filthy trench called 'Mágh Dighi' is the so-called tomb of Ghyasuddin Asam Shah, King of Bengal, and correspondent of the poet Háfiz. This mausoleum formerly consisted of a ponderous stone surrounded by pillars about five feet in height. The stones are all beautifully carved, and the corners of the slabs and the arabesque tracery are as perfect as on the day they left

DISTRICT—continued.

Custody or present use.	Present state of preservation and suggestions for conservation.	Classification.	REMARKS.
6	7	8	9
......	......	...	For account of the ruins of Sonárgaon,—see pages 135 to 139 of Vol. XV of the Archæological Survey Reports.
......	In a ruinous state. The wall surrounding the enclosure has fallen down in places, and several large jungle trees grow close to the tombs, and will ultimately destroy them.	iii	For an account of these tombs, &c., see pages 139 to 145 of Vol. XV of the Archæological Survey Reports.
Abandoned	The tomb has fallen to pieces. The iron clamps that bound the slabs together have rusted, and the roots of trees have undermined the massive stones, some of which are missing. Conservation desirable. The Collector will see if a subscription can be raised for its restoration.	ie	

(16)

(1) DACCA

No.	District.	Locality.	Name of monument.	History or tradition regarding the monument.
1	2	3	4	5
23	Dacca	Maghrápárá, Sonárgaon.		the workman's hands. The stones are hard, almost black, basalt. At the head is a prostrate sandstone pillar half buried in earth. It was apparently used, when erect, as a *cherákdán*, or stand for a light. This tomb ought to be repaired, and the cost of doing so would be inconsiderable. There is no old building in Eastern Bengal which gives a better idea of Muhammadan taste, and there is none which, when properly repaired, would so long defy the ravages of time. The Muhammadans of Sonárgaon are too poor to reconstruct it themselves. They take great pride in showing it, although they know nothing about it but the name of the Sultán who is supposed to be buried there, and they take every care that none of the stones are carried off. It is said that some of the stones were stolen at one time, and the offender was detected and punished with imprisonment.
			Damdamá Fort	The village of Maghrápárá is considered by the natives of Sonárgaon to be the site of the ancient city. It has in its immediate neighbourhood several undoubtedly old buildings, and within a short distance is an eminence, which still bears the name of "Damdamá" or fort. This mound, which has a magnificent tamarind-tree growing on its top, is circular, but no traces of fortifications are visible. It was used for many years by the Muhammadans as their *Ashorkhánd* during the Muharram. On the tenth day all the garlands and ornaments that were made in place of táziyas were here collected to be admired by the people; the practice has died out, as the local Muhammadans have since become Feraxis or non-idolaters.
			Tomb of Munna Shah Darvesh.	In the small market village of Maghrápárá is the tomb of Munna Shah Darvesh. At the foot a light is always burned at night, and every orthodox Muhammadan, as he passes the tomb, stops and mutters a prayer. This saint, about whom nothing is known, is said to have lived at the same time as the more famous pír whose tomb stands a little to the north.
			Tomb of Sheik Mohamed Yasuf (Háfiz Sáheb).	This latter is called the dargá of Sheik Mohamed Yásuf. It contains the tombs of the saint, of his son, and of his wife. It consists of two elongated dome-roofed buildings, each surmounted by two pinnacles or kalas said to have been covered with gold, of which no trace remains. These tombs are destitute of any ornament inside. They are kept scrupulously clean, and are covered with sheets. When a raiyat has reaped an unusually abundant harvest, he presents a few bundles of ripe rice at the tomb in token of gratitude. If any calamity, such as the illness of a member of his

DISTRICT—*continued*.

Custody or present use.	Present state of preservation and suggestions for conservation.	Classification.	REMARKS.
6	7	8	9
......	......	iii	
......	......	iib	
......	......	iib	

(18)

(1) DACCA

No.	District.	Locality.	Name of monument.	History or tradition regarding the monument.
1	2	3	4	5
			Mosque of Mohamed Yasuf.	family, is threatening, he brings rice or bátásá, and prays the saint to avert the affliction. Hindus are as confident of the efficacy of this propitiatory offering, and as frequently employ it, as the Muhammadans. Close to the tombs is a modern masjid, with a khutbá, or inscription, dated A.H. 1112. It was probably erected by pir Mohamed Yasuf. Facing the mosque is a small graveyard enclosed by a brick wall. The graves are numerous, but none are of any importance. Inserted in the wall of the enclosure at the left hand side of the entrance, is a large black stone, measuring two feet by one and a half which most probably belonged to the original or older mosque. The natives believe that if a person has lost any property, he has only to put a coating of lime on this stone, and he will infallibly get the property back. It was covered with a coating of lime when examined in May and June 1895. On scraping off the plaster a beautiful Tughra inscription was found, with the name Jalaluddin Fateh Shah, A.H. 889. This is said to be the oldest inscription discovered in the Dacca district, with the exception of the one in Bábá Adam's Mosque in Rámpal in Bikrampur, which bears the date A.H. 888. Close to the tomb of Mohamed Yasuf is a ruined gateway, called the naubatkháná, where musical instruments were sounded morning and evening, to announce to travellers and fakirs that a place of shelter was at hand. At the back of the modern mosque are the ruins of a house called the tahbise or treasury, where feasts were given by the Superintendent or mutawalli of the mosque. Still further to the north-west are the ruins of the dwellings of the Khwandhars. It is only within late years that this building, which had an upper room at each end, has become uninhabitable. The last residents taught boys to recite the Korán.
24	Dacca	...	Maghrápárá, Sonárgaon.	Tomb of Shah Abdul Ala.	In the mahalla north of Maghrápárá, called Gohaṭṭa, is the tomb of a very celebrated pír, known as Shah Abdul Ala, alias Ponkai Diwanah. It is narrated that he retired to the forest, where he sat for twelve years so absorbed in his devotions that he was unconscious of the lapse of time. When found, he had to be dug out of the mound which the white ants (poka) had raised around him, and which reached to his neck. This pir must have died near the end of the last century, as persons now living knew his son, Shah Imam Bukhsh, alias Chulu Moah. Father and son lie buried close together. At the head of the grave of the former is placed the stone lattice on which he spent his twelve years of meditation. The tombs are otherwise of no interest.

DISTRICT—*continued.*

Custody or present use.	Present state of preservation and suggestions for conservation.	Classification.	REMARKS.
6	7	8	9
......	......	ii*b*	
Abandoned	Exploration desirable ...	iii	

(1) DACCA

No.	District.	Locality.	Name of monument.	History or tradition regarding the monument.
1	2	3	4	5
				They are merely heaps of mud kept carefully clean and covered over with a grass thatch.
				In the same quarter a very large mosque formerly stood, which fell into ruins, when the proprietor sold the bricks to the Hindus of Nárâyanganj. Muhammadans extenuate this offence by asserting that the proprietor, who was a pensioned Deputy Magistrate was insane when he did it. Even the foundations have been dug up. It is said that the walls were 8 feet thick, and that the interior of the mosque was ornamented with carved bricks.
25	Dacca	Maghrápárá Sonárgaon.	Yasuffganj Mosque.	On the roadside, east of Maghrápárá, is a small mosque called the Yasuffganj Masjid. It is a very old one. The walls are nearly 6 feet thick, and this thickness combined with the strength of the masonry has kept the mosque still standing.
26	Do.	Hábibpur, Sonárgaon.	Tomb of Páglá Sáheb.	Beyond the village of Hábibpur, on the right hand side of the district road, is the tomb of "Páglá Sáheb." It is an old insignificant building. Various stories are told of the reason why this pír received such a singular name. One is that he became light-headed, from the intensity of his devotions. Another, that he was a great thief-catcher, who nailed every thief he caught to a wall, and then beheaded him. Having strung several heads together, he threw them into an adjoining khál, which has ever since been known as the "munda málá," i.e., necklace of heads. This tomb is so venerated that parents, Hindu and Muhammadan, offer at it the "choti" or queue of their children when dangerously ill.
27	Do.	Sadipur, Sonárgaon.	Garibulla's Mosque.	This is situated on an elevated mound surrounded by a moat in the village of Sadipur about half a mile north-east of Maghrápárá in the Sonárgaon pargana. It was erected by Sheikh Garibulla, formerly an examiner of cloth, to the East India Company. It bears the date A. H. 1182. Its pinnacles are made of glazed pottery, but the building generally is plain, and devoid of interest.

DISTRICT—*continued.*

Custody or present use.	Present state of preservation and suggestions for conservation.	Classification.	REMARKS.
6	7	8	9
Abandoned	In ruins	iii	
......	Rapidly going to pieces. The dome is covered with pipal trees, the roots of which have penetrated into the masonry.	iii	
......	Overgrown with vegetation and trees, and falling into decay.	iii	
Under the custody of Amir Hossein Mir, an inhabitant of Barsechinish, a neighbouring village, who states that his forefather, Sheikh Garibulla, constructed this mosque.	Although it stands as a witness to the neat, fine, and durable workmanship of old days it is in bad condition and needs repairs. It has lost its parapet, cornices, and the top part of the four pillars at its four corners with the ornamental work thereon. Deep-rooted pipal trees have grown into the walls and the roof. The plaster of the lower parts of the wall has also fallen to the height of about 5′ to 7′ from the plinth level. The mosque does not seem to have received any repairs since its construction. The cost of these repairs roughly estimated will come to about Rs. 250. Nawab Ashannullah has recently provided this amount, and the District Engineer will have the work done shortly.	iii	

(22)

(1) DACCA

No.	District.	Locality.	Name of monument.	History or tradition regarding the monument.
1	2	3	4	5
28	Dacca	Pannam, Sonárgaon.	Dulálpur Bridge	This is a fine Muhammadan bridge over a khál on a village road connecting Pannam with the district road from Hájiganj to Byda Bazar. It has three arches, the middle arch is higher than those at the sides and is intended for the passage of boats. The bridge is very old. The roadway is very steep and is formed of bricks circularly arranged. There is also a smaller bridge leading from the same road over a branch khál to the main street of Pannam village. The roadway of this bridge is also formed of bricks arranged circularly and kept in place by several large pillars of basalt laid flat at the toe or end of the arches. This bridge has towers at its sides which originally flanked a gate-way.
29	Do.	Áminpur, Sonárgaon.	Residence	In Áminpur lie the ruins of the abode of the royal karori, or tax-gatherer. Like all old ruins, they are said to contain fabulous treasures protected by numerous snakes. A descendant of this family whose name is Káli Prasád Karori still resides in the neighbourhood; close to his residence are the ruins of an old Hindu building, the only one existing in Sonárgaon. It is called Jhikoti, and is a building having an elongated domed roof formed of concrete and walls pierced with numerous openings. It was formerly used for religious purposes.
30	Do.	Goaldi, Sonárgaon	Abdul Hámid's mosque.	This is a comparatively modern structure. Its kitaba bears the date A. H. 1116.
31	Do.	Ditto, ditto	Mosque	About a hundred yards to the south of the above is the oldest mosque in Sonárgaon. The residents call this old mosque purána or old mosque. Its kitaba has fallen out, but has been carefully preserved in the interior. On this stone is inscribed the name of Alauddin Husain Shah, A. H. 995. This monarch being an Arab assumed the title Sherif Mecca, but in this inscription he is designated "Hasabi," or Persian from the place of his nativity. The interior of the mosque is 16½ feet square. The four walls, as they ascend, give place to the eight walls of an octagon. At each corner are quarter domes or arches, and the dome rises from the pendentives. As usual there are three mihrabs or arched recesses. The centre one is formed of dark basaltic stones beautifully carved and ornamented with arabesque work. The two side ones are of brick, boldly cut and gracefully arranged. The bricks in the archways have been ground and smoothed by manual labour. The pillars at the doorways are sand-stone, evidently the plunder of some Hindu shrine. Until thirty-four years ago this mosque was used for

DISTRICT—continued.

Custody or present use.	Present state of preservation and suggestions for conservation.	Classification.	REMARKS.
6	7	8	9
Under the custody of Rám Chandra Poddar, Guru Chandra Poddar, and others of Pannam, who are well-to-do men and could easily keep the bridge in good order if so inclined. At present they are doing nothing for the protection or preservation of the bridge. The Collector hopes to get it taken over by the District Board as well as the smaller bridge.	The extremities of the paved roadway of the bridge about 22 feet on each side have sunk a little, but this settlement took place long ago, and there seems to be no danger that it will go further. Some trees have grown into the face of the bridge which should be rooted out. The bridge, has been much affected by the action of saltpetre, and requires repairs. New brickwork is needed in places, and soorkee plaster and pointing are also required. The cost of repairs will be about Rs. 410.	ii*b*	
......	......	iii	
It is used by local worshippers who have abandoned the old one, and it is maintained by the Muhammadan inhabitants of the locality.	In good preservation ...	i*b*	
......	This mosque is built of red brick. Its exterior was formerly ornamented by finely carved bricks in imitation of flowers, but neglect, and the lapse of centuries have left few uninjured.	ii*a*	

(24)

(1) DACCA

No.	District.	Locality.	Name of monument.	History or tradition regarding the monument.
1	2	3	4	5
32	Dacca	Pathorghata, thana Srinagar.	Mosque of Unwar.	worship. The makhadin or servant having died, no care was taken of the building. The dome threatened to fall in, so the worshippers migrated to the modern mosque. The Masjid was built in Hijri 1102, i.e., 207 years ago, by one Unwar, a courtier of Emperor Alamgir Shah (Aurangzeb), and bears an inscription in front. It is 34′ × 20′ outside measurement, has one central dome and a smaller one on each side.
33	Do.	Rájbári, thána Munshiganj.	Maṭh (tower)	It is situated about 2 miles to the south-west of the Rájbári outpost. It is a monumental tower of brick masonry built, it is said, over the funeral pyre of the mother of Chánd Rayya and Kedár Rayya who were about 300 years ago some independent princes of the locality. It is known as the Rájbári maṭh. It measures 30 feet square at base and about 80 feet in height and has a small room within it. The dimensions of the maṭh are large and its proportions elegant. It stands up as a conspicuous landmark visible for many miles across the Ganges on the south and the Megná on the north. The passenger steamers passing up and down the Ganges between Dacca and Goalundo have this maṭh in sight for 4 or 5 hours, with an interval in the middle, as they pass it first going down the Ganges, and afterwards again after rounding the point at the junction of the rivers, as they get up the Megná.
34	Do.	Rámpál, thána Munshiganj.	Bábá Adam's tomb and mosque.	The tomb is a common plastered brick sarcophagus, standing on a platform 25 feet square. The mosque is the only old building in Rámpál. Its outside measurements are 49 feet long by 38 feet wide and the inside measures 33′ × 22′. There is a tradition that the Burmese during their invasion took away the large pieces of stone from the corners of the walls, the jambs of the doors and the springing points of the domes. There is a stone inscription on the front of the building in a character no one in the neighbourhood can decipher. Tradition gives the date of erection as A. H. 888 or 424 years ago.
35	Do.	Mirkadim, thána Munshiganj.	The Ballál bridge.	This is a strong structure of masonry and stands upon the Mirkadim khál. It is said to have been built by Rájá Ballál Sen before the conquest of Bengal

DISTRICT—*continued.*

Custody or present use.	Present state of preservation and suggestions for conservation.	Classification.	REMARKS.
6	7	8	9
It is now under the charge of a Mollah or priest by name Jiban Khan, who lives near the mosque and enjoys an annual rent of Rs. 12-2 and the product of two pieces of rent-free pirottar land. It is used for daily prayer, and the above income goes to meet the expenses of lighting and mats, &c., that are used during the prayers.	It is in a good state of preservation and is said to have been repaired to some extent about 20 years ago by one of the inhabitants of the locality who is now in indigent circumstances. The late repairs have greatly improved the mosque, but some plants need rooting out, and some doors and repairs to floor are required. The cost of the repairs will come to about Rs. 250. Nawab Ashannullah Bahádur has supplied the amount, and the District Engineer is having the work done.	ii*b*	
It is not a place of worship and not in the custody of any particular person or used for any particular object.	It is neglected and much dilapidated. Large trees have grown in the masonry, and some of them have borne fruit. Saltpetre has also eaten away the plaster. It is only the strength of the masonry which has kept the Mot still standing. It has been estimated that the cotton trees can be eradicated and the pointing renewed for Rs. 700, towards which the Collector has raised Rs. 500. The District Engineer will see the work done.	i*a*	
The mosque is in charge of Ainuddin Khandkar, Muhammad Fairuddin Khandkar, and Mafizuddin Dewan, who live near the mosque and enjoy the produce of about 10 bighás of rent-free land for its maintenance. It is still used for worship and is much revered as a sacred place in the neighbourhood.	It is in a very dilapidated state. It has two stone pillars in the centre, which with the surrounding walls support a roof with six domes. Three of these domes have almost entirely fallen in, another is severely shattered, and the two last are intact. The whole of the building is overgrown with large trees, the roots of which have penetrated deep into the masonry, and the building cannot be repaired.	iii	See pages 132 to 135 of Vol. XV of the Archæological Survey Reports.
It is still used by pedestrians who cross the bridge over the narrow top of the wing walls.	The two south wings have fallen down, and the cut-waters are cracked. The whole structure	ii*b*	

22535

(1) DACCA

No.	District.	Locality.	Name of monument.	History or tradition regarding the monument.
1	2	3	4	5
36	Dacca	Táltollah, tháná Srinagar.	Bridge	by the Muhammadans. If this is correct, it is about 800 years old. It consists of a centre Gothic arch 14 feet span and 28 feet in height above the bed of the khál, with two side arches of 7 feet 3 inches span each, and 17 feet high. It is a fine bridge. The piers are 6 feet thick. The wings are straight back, and the whole length of the bridge is 173 feet. The abutments, piers, and arches, and the two north wings are entire. This bridge is also said to have been built by Rájá Ballál Sen. It is over the Táltollah khál. The capital of the Hindu Rájás was at Rámpál about two miles to the east of Munshiganj. Both this and the Mirkadim bridge stand in a direct line westward from the capital, over two parallel khála, and it is said that they stood on a line of road running from the capital westward to the bank of the Pádma river. It consisted of three arches of masonry, of which 2 were of 15 feet opening each and the other of 30 feet. The larger arch was blown up by gunpowder during the first years of the English rule, so as to secure direct communication between Calcutta and Dacca, for large boats for the conveyance of troops, &c., to the Eastern frontier and for the Burmese wars.

(2) MYMENSINGH

37	Mymensingh	Goiyaripa near Sherpur, in Jámálpur subdivision.	Fort ruins	An old fort built of mud. It has no architectural pretensions, but is of considerable size. It was built not less than 350 years, (and probably about 500 years) ago as an outpost, it is said, to check the incursions of the hill tribes. It is encompassed by three walls divided by two ditches, one between the outer and middle and the other between the middle and inner walls. There are four gates on the four sides of the fort. The east gate is called Koomdoodri; the west gate is called Panidoodri; the south gate Syám Shakarudoodri, and the north gate Khirtidoodri. Two pieces of stone are lying near the Panidoodri, and they are supposed to be a part of a door. A tombstone of Amir Hushen Sháh still stands within the fort. A big stone with an inscription in Arabic characters, which was placed on the tomb, was taken to the Asiatic Society, Calcutta in 1871. There is a boat-shaped island between the southern and western interior ditches called by some "Kosha" and by others "Dingé." There are several ponds within the fort, of which the Mati Miab Talao is well known. It is said that a powerful hillman lived in this place who would

DISTRICT—concluded.

Custody or present use.	Present state of preservation and suggestions for conservation.	Classification.	REMARKS.
6	7	8	9
The fort, however, is very dangerous.	is overgrown with large trees which have taken root in the masonry. The bridge needs thorough repairs, which will cost about 8,000 rupees. With such repairs the structure would be worth about 50,000 rupees, and the Collector thinks the work should be undertaken by the District Board.		
It is still used by people of the neighbourhood, who walk with extreme danger over the shattered arches and a light and narrow wooden footpath thrown across the demolished arch.	The gunpowder has totally destroyed the larger arch, and has so much shattered the other two arches and the piers that the restoration of the bridge is hopeless.	iii	

DISTRICT.

No custodian	In a ruinous state, and there is nothing about it worth preserving.	iii	

(28)

(2) MYMENSINGH

No.	District.	Locality.	Name of monument.	History or tradition regarding the monument.
1	2	3	4	5
				oppress travellers, and one Humaun Sha Amir killed him and built a fort here. Other say that Humaun Sha Amir, who was a nephew of the Emperor of Delhi, took refuge here from fear of the Emperor. During the quarrel between the Rájá of Kuch Bihár and Patkoor the Governor of Bengal, Mánsingha, put up here for a short time. The following is a copy of the translation made by the late Professor Blochmann of the stone inscription in the possession of the Asiatic Society :— "In the name of God, the merciful, the clement! There is no God but Allah. Mahomed is Allah's prophet * * * There is no God but Allah *. Mahomed is Allah's prophet * * O God, bless Mahomed, the elected, and Ali, the chosen, and Fatimah the pure, and Hasan * and Hussain * * built * the King of the age and the period Saifuddunaja Waddin Abdul Muzaffar Firoz Shah, the King— May God perpetuate his kingdom and his rule! This (vault) was completed in the blessed * Ramjan 8 * * *." The slab of this inscription was in the Museum of the Asiatic Society, Calcutta having been sent down by Babu Hari Chandra Chaudhuri of Sherpur. It is of granite and measures 4 feet by 2 feet, but the letters are very indistinct, and many are hopelessly broken away. The inscription seems to have belonged to a vault. In each corner of the slab is a square, containing the name of one of the first khalifas ; the two squares on the left and those on the right are joined by vertical lines, but the letters between each set of squares are illegible. The slab was entire, but an elephant put his foot on it, and the right side of the stone broke in two. The inscription itself consists of only four lines. This shows that the vault to which this inscription belonged was constructed in the reign of the Emperor Firoz Shah, who ruled from 1351 to 1388. This monarch is said to have been celebrated for his public works, and this fort was probably one of those works.
39	Mymensingh	Keshoregange	Temple of Lakshi Náráyaṇ.	This temple consisting of 21 pinnacled structures, together with other adjoining buildings, viz. (1) the Jaltungi (summer house), (2) the Rásbári, (3) the Durgá mandir, (4) the Sib Mandir, and other smaller structures was erected about 150 year ago and are all dedicated to the god Lakshmi Náráyaṇ. They are known by the common name of Deb Mandir. Four tanks were also dug. One of these was a large piece of water, 265 yards in length by 142 yards in breadth. It is situated on the east of the temple of Lakshmi-Náráyaṇ. The Jaltungi or three-storied building rises from the bed of the tank in question. The temple of Lakshmi Náráyaṇ and its adjoining buildings cover an area of 9,216 square feet. There are two inscriptions in Sanskrit in the big temple, a considerable height from the base. Some of the letters are obliterated.

DISTRICT—concluded.

Custody or present use.	Present state of preservation and suggestions for conservation.	Classification.	REMARKS.
6	7	8	9
In the custody of Babus Lalit Bihári Roy and Rám Kumár Dás.	Two of the buildings are in ruins.	iib	

(30)

(3) FARIDPUR

No.	District.	Locality.	Name of monument.	History or tradition regarding the monument.
1	2	3	4	5
39	Faridpur	Khábáshpur, thání Faridpur.	Mosque	Built by the great-grandfather of one Meherálí Khundakar of Khábáshpur, who was known as a fakir or darvesh amongst the people of his time.
40	Ditto	Makahámi, thání Baliakandi.	Temple of Bangáa Gopál.	Built about 200 years ago by one Ajodhyárám Sen of the Baidya caste and dedicated to the family deity Bangáa Gopáljí.
41	Ditto	Bathamari, thání Maksudpur.	Temple	Built about 100 years ago by one Subodha Roy, forefather of Jajñeśvar Sáhá of Bathamari. He intended to set up a Hindu idol named Siva in the temple, but did not succeed in doing so.
42	Ditto	Chucha, thání Maksudpur.	Dolmañcha temple.	Built about 70 or 80 years ago by one Padma Lochan Datta of Chucha for performing the Doljátrá. It is known as Dolmañcha.
43	Ditto	Pathrail, thání Bhañga.	Mosque of Abda Khandakar.	Built about more than 200 years ago by one Abda Khandakar of Pathrail for the purposes of namas or prayer.
44	Ditto	Azampur, thání Pangsa.	Mosque of Nasir Shaik.	Said to have been built some 200 years ago by one Nasir Shaik, a kotwal in the service of Rájá Rámjíban Roy of Nator, when the parganá Balgáchi was included in the zamindari of the Rájá.
45	Ditto	Mathurápur, thání Balgáchi.	Temple	Said to have been built about 200 years ago by one Sañgrám Shah of the Baidya family for dedication to some deity, but as one of the masons employed in its construction accidentally fell down from the steeple and died, it was abandoned.
46	Ditto	Dhobádáñgá, thání Bhusbana.	Temples of Madan Mohan and Kessab.	Built about 300 years ago by one Durlabh Chandra Shaha of Dhobádáñgá. Two Hindu idols, one named Madan Mohan Thákur and the other thákur Kessab, were worshipped in these two temples. At the time of the Doljátrá and the Rásjátrá, two Hindu festivals, many people used to gather at the place, and the ceremonies were performed with great éclat.
47	Ditto	Naliá Jámálpore, thání Baliákándi.	Temple of Jayá Durgá.	Built about 100 years ago by one Krishna Rám Chakravarti of Naliá and dedicated to the goddess Jayá Durgá.

(4) BACKERGUNGE

| 48 | Backergunge | Bibi Chini, outpost Niámati. | Bibi Chini's Mosque. | An old mosque raised on an artificial mound of considerable size and height. It is said to have been built by Bibi Chini, sister of Niyamatullah, who founded Niámati, and is evidently a relic of the time when the Muhammadans first settled in the district. It remained hidden in the jungle for centuries and was discovered at the time when the Sundarbans were cultivated. |

DISTRICT.

Custody or present use.	Present state of preservation and suggestions for conservation.	Classification.	REMARKS.
6	7	8	9
In charge of Meherâli Khundakar of Khâbâshpur and not used for any purpose.	In a dilapidated state. Is not much taken care of. Requires repairs.	ii*b*	
The present owner is Basanta Kumár Sen. The temple has now been abandoned.	Overgrown with trees. Cost of repairs beyond the means of the present owner.	ii*b*	
In charge of Jâjneśvar Sáhá, but not used for any purpose.	Plants have grown over the top of the temple. Requires repairs and whitewashing.	ii*b*	
In charge of Nirmala Sundarí, daughter of Ráj Kumár Datta of Chucha. Not used for any purpose.	Has been broken in places and is overgrown with jungle. Repairs required.	ii*b*	
In charge of Abdul Rexxaquo, son of Khandakar Neyaxuddin, but not used at present.	Ditto ditto ...	ii*b*	
The present owners are the zamindars of Belgáchi, Maulavi Faiz Bux Chowdhury and others.	In a bad state of repairs and overgrown with trees. The present owners are well able to undertake the necessary repairs.	ii*b*	
The present owner is Súryakumár Lahiri of Korokdi.	In a ruined state overgrown with trees. The steeple has come down. The present owner is well able to pay for substantial repairs.	ii*b*	
In charge of Mathurá Náth Sáhá and Dino Náth Sáhá of Dhobádáñgá. The idols have now been removed from these temples and they are not used for any purpose.	Both temples are broken in places and are surrounded by jungle. Require repairs.	ii*b*	
The present owners are Sashí Bhúshan Chakravartí and others of Naliá.	In a ruined state and the owners are not able to make the necessary repairs.	ii*b*	

DISTRICT.

Is situated in the zamindari of Babu Lála Hájendra Kumár Singh Chaudhari, of Bakshi Bazar, Dacca, and is in his khás possession. Is not used in any way now.	Ruined	ii*b*	

(4) BACKERGUNGE

No.	District.	Locality.	Name of monument.	History or tradition regarding the monument.
1	2	3	4	5
49	Backergunge	Koshba, thána Gour nadí.	Mosque of Sabi Khán.	Built by the man known as Sabi Khán. It is considerably superior in architectural merit to Bibi Chini's mosque. Its roof is supported by four stone pillars, which must have been brought from a great distance. There is a curious belief in the locality that of the four stone pillars which support the dome, one gradually decays and is reduced in size. After a few months the pillar again gradually reaches its original dimensions while another pillar decays. This process goes on in the four pillars. To test this legend the District Engineer, according to the Collector's instructions, has taken dimensions of the pillars as he found them on the 11th April 1895. These dimensions will be checked on his next visit.

DISTRICT—*concluded.*

Custody or present use.	Present state of preservation and suggestions for conservation.	Classification.	REMARKS.
6	7	8	9
Is in the custody of Kazi Golám Mastafá, *alias* Madh Kázi.	Ruinous	iib	

DACCA DIVISION.

Geographical Index to Ancient Monuments.

District.	Village.	Description of monument.	Page.
1	2	3	4
Backergunge	Bibi Chini	Bibi Chini's *Mosque*	80
	Kodhba	*Mosque* of Sabi Khán	82
Dacca	Amínpur	Residence	22
	Dacca	Págla *bridge*	10
		Tangi do.	10
		The great katra (*Caravansarai*)	4
		The small do. (*Caravansarai*)	4
		The *chok* (market-place)	4
		Armenian *Church* of the Holy Resurrection	6
		The Lálbágh *fort*	2
		Idgah of Mir Abdul Kasim	4
		Bibi Peri's *mausoleum*	2
		Mosque and *tomb* of Hajji Kabjeh Shahabag	4 & 6
		The Sát Gombá *mosque*	10
		Hussoni Dalan *palace*	2
		Temple of Dhákeśvari	4
		Do. of Jayakáli	6
		Do. of Siva	6
		Tomb of Colombo Sáheb	8
		Tombs of Nawabs Nasurat-jang, Samsadwalá, Kamaralawalá, Gáziuddin Hydar.	2
		Tomb of Shah Ali Saheb	10
		Do. in Shahbag Park	6
	Goaldi	Abdul Hámid's *Mosque*	22
		Mosque	22
	Hábibpur	Tomb of Páglá Sáheb	20
	Hájigaáj	*Fort*	12
	Maghrápárá	Dumdamá *Fort*	16
		Mohamed Yasuf's *mosque*	18
		Yasuffgaúj *Mosque*	20
		Tomb of Musna Shah Darvesh	16
		" Shah Abdul Alá	18
		" Shaik Mohamed Yasuf	16
	Mirkadim	Valláli *Bridge*	24
	Munshiganj	*Fort*	12
	Náligañj	Kadam Rasul *Fort* and *Mosque*	12
	Panam	Dulálpur *Bridge*	22
	Páthorghátá	*Mosque* of Unwar	24
	Rájbári	Math (*tower*)	24
	Rámpál	Bábá Adam's *tomb* and *mosque*	24
	Sadipur	Garibulla's *Mosque*	20
	Soukhanda	*Fort* ruins	12
	Sonargaon	Tombs of five pirs (saints)	14
		Tomb of Ghyasuddin Asam Shah	14
	Taltollah	*Bridge*	26
Faridpur	Azampur	*Mosque* of Nasir Shaik	30
	Bathamari	*Temple*	30
	Churha	Dolmanchia *temple*	30
	Dhobádángá	Temples of Kesab	30
		Do. of Madan Mohan	30
	Khabashpur	*Mosque*	30
	Mathurápur	*Temple*	30
	Mekahami	Do. of Rangu Gopál	30
	Nalia Jamalpur	Do. of Jaya Durgá	30
	Pashrail	*Mosque* of Abda Khandakar	30
Mymensingh	Goiyaripa	*Fort* ruins	26
	Keshoregunge	Temple of Lakshi Nárayan	28

DACCA DIVISION.

Index of Ancient Monuments by classes.

1		2	3	4
Classification of Building.		District.	Village.	Page.
Bridges	Dulálpur	Dacca	Pannam	22
	Páglá	Do.	Dacca	10
	Taltolish	Do.	Taltolla	26
	Tungi	Do.	Dacca	10
	Valláli	Do.	Mirkadim	24
		Do.	Dacca	4
Chak (market-place).				
Churches	Armenian Church of the Holy Resurrection.	Do.	Do.	6
Forts	Dundomá	Do.	Maghrápárá	16
		Do.	Hájígánj	12
	Kadam Rasul	Do.	Náligánj	12
	Lalbagh	Do.	Ditto	8
		Mymensingh	Goíyaripa	26
		Dacca	Munshígánj	12
		Do.	Sondikhanda	12
Idgah	Mir Abdul Kassim's	Do.	Dacca	4
Katras (caravanserais).	Mir Abdul Kassim's (great)	Do.	Do.	4
	Nawab Shaista Khan's (small).	Do.	Do.	4
Mausoleum	Bíbí Peri's	Do.	Do.	2
Mosques	Abda Khandakar's	Faridpur	Pathrail	20
	Abdul Hámid's	Dacca	Goaldi	22
	Bábá Adam's	Do	Rámpál	24
	Bibi Chini's	Backergunge	Bibi Chini	20
	Gambulla's	Dacca	Sadipur	20
		Do.	Goaldi	22
	Haji Khajeh Shahabag's	Do.	Dacca	4
	Kadam Rasul	Do.	Náligánj	12
		Faridpur	Khabashpur	20
	Mohamed Yasuf's	Dacca	Maghrápárá	16
	Nasir Shaik's	Faridpur	Azampur	20
	Sabi Khan's	Backergunge	Koshba	32
	Sat Gomal	Dacca	Dacca	10
	Unwar's	Do.	Páthaoghátá	24
	Yesufíganj	Do.	Maghrápárá	20
Palace	Husseni Dalan's	Do.	Dacca	2
Residence		Do.	Aminpur	22
Temples	Bangas Gopál	Faridpur	Makrhani	30
		Ditto	Botkamari	30
	Dhákesvári	Dacca	Dacca	4
	Dolmañcha	Faridpur	Chucha	30
	Jayakáli	Dacca	Dacca	6
	Jaya Durgá	Faridpur	Nalia Jamalpur	30
	Kesub	Ditto	Dhobádángá	30
	Lakshi Náráyan	Keshoregaunge	Mymensingh	28
	Madan Mohan	Ditto	Dhobádángá	30
		Ditto	Mathurápur	30
	Siva	Dacca	Dacca	6
Tombs	Bábá Adam's	Do.	Rámpál	24
	Colombo Saheb's	Do.	Dacca	8
		Do.	Do.	4
	Five Pirs'	Do.	Sonargaon	14
	Ghyasuddin Azam Shah	Do.	Ditto	14
	Haji Khajeh Shahabag's	Do.	Dacca	6
	Munna Shah Darvesh's	Do.	Maghrápárá	16
	Nawab Gaziuddin Hyder's	Do.	Dacca	2
	Nawab Kamaradawala's	Do.	Do.	2
	Nawab Nasratjang's	Do.	Do.	2
	Nawab Samandwala's	Do.	Do.	2
	Páglá Saheb's	Do.	Bábíbpur	20
	Shah Abdul Ala's	Do.	Maghrápárá	18
	Shah Ali Saheb's	Do.	Dacca	10
	Shaik Mohamed Yasuf's	Do.	Maghrápárá	16
Tower (mash)		Do.	Rajbari	24

www.ingramcontent.com/pod-product-compliance
Lightning Source LLC
Chambersburg PA
CBHW022147090426
42742CB00010B/1418